MANY WAYS TO LEARN

Young People's Guide
to Learning Disabilities

☆ ☆ ☆

JUDITH M. STERN, M.A.

AND

UZI BEN-AMI, Ph.D.

Illustrations by

MICHAEL CHESWORTH

MAGINATION PRESS • NEW YORK

To our parents, who inspired us to learn and to teach:
Alexander and Shoshana Ben-Ami and Raula Stern,
and to the memory of Bernard Stern.

Library of Congress Cataloging-in-Publication Data

Stern, Judith M.
    Many ways to learn: young people's guide to learning disabilities
/ Judith Stern and Uzi Ben-Ami; illustrations by Michael Chesworth.
    p. cm.
    Includes bibliographical references.
    Summary: Provides information on learning disabilities and
strategies for coping with the problem and leading a successful life.
    ISBN 0-945354-74-6
    1. Learning disabilities—Juvenile literature. 2. Learning
disabled children—Education—Juvenile literature. 3. Study skills—
Juvenile literature. [1. Learning disabilities.] I. Ben-Ami,
Uzi. II. Chesworth, Michael, ill. III. Title.
LC4704.S75 1996
371.9—dc20   96-30478
                                                                   CIP
                                                                    AC

Photographs by Phyllis D. Elpern, except those on pages 4, 7, 9, and 36.

The authors are grateful for Dr. Patricia Quinn's contributions to the chapter
on the brain. Dori Friedman and Heidi Parker Morris generously shared
their expertise in developing the chapter on computers and the software list.
Our skillful and patient editor, Susan Kent Cakars, served as our own mountain guide.

Published by
MAGINATION PRESS
An imprint of Brunner/Mazel, Inc.
19 Union Square West, New York, NY 10003

Manufactured in the United States of America

10 9 8 7 6 5 4 3 2 1

CONTENTS

Foreword for Parents

Along with all the pleasures of parenting, there is also plenty of hard work. Parenting is even harder when you have to watch your child struggle with learning difficulties. As a parent, you can provide a supportive environment and useful assistance at home, but you cannot take away the disappointment and hurt that are almost an inevitable part of your child's school experience. You may ask yourself if there is anything else that can be done. The answer is a resounding "yes." There is a great deal that can be done by you, by the school, and most importantly by your child.

This book is written for young people with learning disabilities. Reading it will help them learn to help themselves. The book provides a clear and positive understanding of what it means to have a learning disability. Learning Disabilities affect school performance. Therefore, we discuss the school's definition, which emphasizes deficits in specific school subjects. In this way, the book is directly relevant to your child's academic life.

Most children wonder about the connection between their intelligence and their learning disability. In order to calm their fears and address some common concerns, we discuss intelligence and the brain's role in learning. These topics are perplexing, even for professionals. *We chose clarity over complexity*, so that children can begin to explore the concepts without becoming overwhelmed.

Helping your child learn how to compensate for learning disabilities is the next step you can take. We provide a variety of practical suggestions for learning in school and everyday life. Once your children discover techniques and materials that work for them, they gain in self-esteem and optimism.

Perhaps the most potent message children with learning disabilities can take from this book is that their strengths will be what carry them through. This is where parents come in most significantly. As you nurture and encourage your children, you will continually help them look for all that they *can* do. No matter the age of your learning disabled child, you will be the guide part way up the mountain of effort and achievement. Patience and support will be your tools. A positive attitude, realistic information, creativity, and a well-grounded understanding will be your child's tools.

May you enjoy that part of the climb that you take together.

PART I

UNDERSTANDING LEARNING DISABILITIES

1 ☆
INTRODUCTION

Coping with a learning disability may feel like climbing a mountain. Many times the path will seem rocky and difficult. You may feel lost or confused. But there is a lot of pleasure in climbing. You can enjoy the scenery, look down and admire how far up you have come, and feel proud of how strong and capable you really are.

When you begin to climb, you may look up and see how far you have to go. The distance may seem overwhelming. The equipment you carry may feel heavy and uncomfortable. But your desire to reach your goal will help you find the way. Your positive attitude and effort will help. You will also start to figure out many ways to make your climb easier and fun. After a while, you realize that you *will* make it.

Climbing together with an experienced guide will help you as you go. Parents, teachers, and counselors are good guides. Good friends will encourage you when the path becomes rough. They will also share the good times with you. Having company is the best way to go.

There are many ways to climb a mountain. There are many ways to learn and enjoy going through school. This book is your guide to getting started.

If you are reading this book, someone has probably told you that you have a learning disability. If you have a learning disability, one of the best things you can do for yourself is to find out what it means. Then you can take steps to help yourself.

Try to read this book with your mind wide open. You may already know some of the information. Some ideas may be new to you. Some parts of the book will not apply to you, and you may choose to skip over those parts. However, before you say, "That's not me," you may want to check it out. You may learn something new and helpful. If something is not clear, ask someone else what it means. Parents, teachers, and counselors can help with this. If you find information that seems especially important to you, make a note of it so you can continue to think about it later.

We have worked with many children who have learning disabilities. We hope to share with you what these kids have in common, and how wonderfully different each one is.

We believe that one of the most important parts of understanding *your* learning disability is to look at all that you *can* do. This book will help you to find your strengths. It will also help you realize that there are many good ways to improve your ability to learn.

What Is a Learning Disability?

A simple way to describe it is to say that **if you have great difficulty learning a school subject, even though your intelligence is average or above, you may have a learning disability.** The following chapters will tell you all about learning disabilities: what they are, how to tell when you have them, what it is like to have them, and most important, what to do about them.

5

Who Has Learning Disabilities?

Millions of people around the country and all over the world have learning disabilities. In the United States alone, more than 2,000,000 children have some form of learning disability. Both girls and boys have learning disabilities, and adults have them, too.

The famous scientist Albert Einstein had a learning disability in reading. He did not learn to read until he was eight years old. He was *very* good in science and in math. However, when he was a child, his teachers thought that he would never be able to read well or finish school. Even a genius such as Albert Einstein was very good at some of his studies, but had difficulty learning other things. **Albert Einstein did not give up, and he did learn how to read, although it was not easy for him.** When he grew up, he invented the Theory of Relativity and changed the way we now understand the universe.

2★

ONE PERSON'S STORY

My name is Alexander Ian Papolos. I am ten years old and I have a learning disability. This is not something you catch. There is nothing physically wrong with me. It just means that I can't read or write well. I have a mild case, but I still have a lot of trouble reading and writing.

I knew that I could not read since I was five. When I was a little child, I never showed any interest in TV shows that would help me read and write. I never wanted to read and write. I had to be tricked into it, or people had to push me into it. I always pushed away from reading and writing and dictated my thoughts to another person, as I am doing right now.

When I see some words, it's like I'm staring into a black hole. When I open a book and see how many pages there are and the small print, I get freaked out, and I try to avoid reading that book. My heart starts to beat a little faster, and I do not like to feel that way. But it automatically happens.

Being smart in most subjects is a downfall with a learning disability. People see my grades for the things I'm good at, and they think I am a very good student. But then, when they see my grades for reading and language arts, the tables turn. They think I'm not the smart kid that they thought I was. Now they think that I am a stupid, lazy kid.

When I am sitting in the middle of a class and they ask me to read something out loud and I can't pronounce or read something, my classmates say the words for me, all at once, very slowly. This is frustrating and embarrassing. They do it because they think I cannot read at all.

When we play "Say–Spell–Say," if you do it correctly, you win a prize. But no one ever wants to be matched up with me. They think I can never get the word right. Actually, I often do know the words.

I was not happy and not sad when I found out that I had a learning disability. But it was a relief to find out that I wasn't stupid. I feel that I am disabled. Whenever I look at a word I don't know, I change it into a word that I do know that sounds similar. Other times, I just don't know. I look at the words and feel locked out. I'm happy that I am only disabled in two subjects: reading and spelling.

I know that I'm getting better, but I feel that I will never be able to read as well as my friends. It's very hard to watch kids who aren't so bright reading better than I can. Every day I learn a little more to help me read. By trying over and over again, reading with teachers and family, I improve a little. I am told that every journey begins with a first step.

The way I deal with my self-esteem is to think about the things I'm very good in, such as science, math, and physical activities. Some days I'm laughed at in school by certain people, and some people look at me in disgust. But I look back at them and think that if they do that to a person like me, they are much worse off than I am. That is what the world is about: Everyone hiding

their disabilities and trying to think they have none themselves.

It's very hard to go through a day with people making fun of you, but then I think of the things I'm good at (and others aren't), and that gets me through.

Sometimes I'm afraid that I will not be able to graduate, but I know I will overcome. Those are just negative thoughts. My mother assures me that I will, and mostly I believe her, except for the faint feelings that I have. For example, when people laugh at me or I am sitting in front of someone I like or would like to impress, I try so hard not to mess up. I just stare into the word and try to get it out. It looks like I'm entering some hypnotic world. I don't understand why it is so hard. But I do not feel sorry for myself, because I know there are much worse-off souls.

The good things about being learning disabled are that I am much more sensitive to people who have disabilities and I have unlimited time in a testing situation. I understand that colleges would like to have a student who has a learning disability and pulled himself up and improved.

Sometimes it goes through my mind that I would switch places with someone who is not learning disabled in a hot second, but then I think of things that I am good in and that others are not, and I accept my life as a human being.

This is all true, and this is what it's like for me to have a learning disability.

3 ⭐
HOW DO YOU KNOW IF YOU HAVE A LEARNING DISABILITY?

Everyone has different ways of learning. These are called *learning styles* or *learning differences*. Most kids can learn school subjects well using their own learning styles. But if you have had a **serious difficulty** for a long time with learning language, reading, writing, or math in school and you have average or above average **intelligence,** you may have a learning disability.

Because the definition of learning disability includes having average or above average intelligence, one of the first things your school looks at is your intelligence.

What Is Intelligence?

Intelligence is your ability to figure out answers to new problems and new ways to do things, not only in school but everywhere else. Intelligence is also your ability to understand and learn.

Intelligence shows itself in many ways. When you help your parents figure out how to move a very large sofa through a small door, you show intelligence. When you figure out by yourself how to fix a video camera, you show intelligence. When you find good words and ideas to defend yourself in an argument, you show intelligence. When you think up a quicker route home from your friend's house, you show intelligence. When you figure out a play in football or create a new dance, you show intelligence.

You can be very intelligent in many ways, but still be unable to learn certain subjects quickly or well in school.

Intelligence Tests

Intelligence tests are used to estimate *how well and how quickly you learn new things taught in school.* Intelligence tests are also called **IQ tests,** because at the end of the test you receive an IQ (intelligence quotient) score.

Most people have average IQ scores. If you have an average IQ, it means that some people scored lower, some people scored higher, and you scored in the middle. If you are considered learning disabled, your IQ must be *at least* average. So do not believe anyone who teases you about your intelligence. **You are as smart or smarter than the other kids around you.**

If your IQ scores are VERY high, but your reading, math, or written language skills are below your grade level, the school may call you **gifted learning disabled,** because you are unable to learn as well as would be expected with such a high IQ.

Intelligence tests do not tell how smart you are in all areas of your life. IQ scores do not tell how well you can do outside of school or how well you will succeed in life. They do not tell how hard you can work. They do not tell how well you listen or how organized you are in school. They tell nothing about how good a friend you are, or how well you do in sports or art. Intelligence tests cannot tell how well you speak or sing or dance. All of these can be just as important in life as doing well in school subjects. To succeed in life, you need to know how to solve problems and how to work well with people.

Serious Difficulty

As we have said, in school you are called learning disabled only *if you have average or above average intelligence, and have had* **a serious difficulty** *for a long time with learning language, math, reading or writing.* What do we mean when we say "a serious difficulty?"

Here is an example. If you are in the sixth grade, and your IQ scores are average, but you can do only fourth grade math, you would probably be considered learning disabled in math. Being two grades behind in math is considered a serious difficulty.

Other Learning Disabilities Tests

Along with the IQ test, other tests are done to see if you have learning disabilities. Special tests are given in reading, writing, and math. Your language, listening, memory, copying, attention, and work speed are usually checked. You will probably be asked how you feel about yourself and about school. Kids usually enjoy this kind of testing. Your teachers and parents are also asked for information. All the test results and other information are then put together to see if you have a learning disability.

School Meetings

Once all the testing is done, your parents, teachers, guidance counselor, principal, and school psychologist get together in a school meeting to decide if you need special help. If they agree that you have a learning disability, they will make a plan for how to teach you best. This is sometimes called an IEP, or **Individualized Educational Plan.**

4 ☆
DIFFERENT KINDS OF LEARNING DISABILITIES

Usually schools name learning disabilities by the subjects that cause difficulty. For example, if your serious difficulty is in reading, you have a reading disability. It is possible to be learning disabled in more than one subject. The learning disabilities we talk about in this book are:

> **Reading disability**
>
> **Math disability**
>
> **Written language disability**
>
> **Oral language disability**

Reading Disability

If you have a reading disability, you may have a few or many of the following problems:

✔ You may reverse letters (such as read a **b** for a **d**).
✔ You may skip over words or sentences.

✔ You may read very slowly.

✔ You may need more time than other students to learn to read well.

✔ You may have trouble sounding out words. You may not be able to remember the sounds of letters. It may be hard for you to put the sounds together.

✔ You may have trouble recognizing words, even though you have seen them many times.

✔ You may look at a word and read it as another word that looks nearly the same. For example, if the word is **where,** you may read **were,** or you may read **burnt** as **burst.**

✔ You may have trouble understanding what you read, even if you can read all the words correctly.

Some people use the word *dyslexia* to describe difficulties in being able to read.

What can be done?

👍 You may learn better by sounding out most words letter by letter, and sound by sound.

You may learn better when you memorize whole words at a time. That way you will not need to sound them out each time you see them.

 You may learn new words by reading the rest of the sentences around a word, and then figuring out that word.

Math Disability

If you have a math disability, you may have a few or many of the following problems:

✔ You may not learn math facts as quickly or easily as other children. You may need lots of practice before you can understand new math ideas.

✔ You may not be able to understand math problems well enough to figure out how to solve them.

✔ You may have difficulty memorizing. This makes it hard to remember math facts.

✔ You may have trouble working on math problems that require several steps.

✔ You may make mistakes because you work too quickly and make careless errors.

What can be done?

 You may learn better by using things you can see and touch with your hands, like dried beans, blocks, or calculators.

👍 You may learn your math facts by practicing them on the computer or listening to them on a tape, over and over.

👍 You may work in a small math group, where the teacher can give you more help.

👍 You may understand math problems better if a teacher draws a picture of the problem.

Written Language Disability

If you have a written language disability, you may have a few or many of the following problems:

✔ You may have difficulty holding a pen or pencil and writing clear, neat letters.

✔ Your work may be difficult for others to read, and you may often erase what you have written.

✔ You may have good ideas, but you may not be able to organize them one after the other. You may not be able to put your thoughts on paper in a way that other people can understand.

✔ You may make many errors, like not using capital letters, correct punctuation, or complete sentences when you write.

What can be done?

👍 Cursive writing may be easier for you than printing, since the letters flow into each other.

👍 Try skipping lines when you write, so your work is easier to read.

👍 Erasable pens make it easy to make corrections.

👍 Your hand may feel less tired if you use very smooth pens. If you hold your pen or pencil tightly, have someone teach you how to hold it correctly. Rubber pencil grips can also help.

👍 Outlining and webbing can help you organize ahead what you will write. (See page 63.)

👍 Computers can be a great help. (See chapter 9.)

Oral Language Disability

If you have an oral language difficulty, you may have a few or many of the following problems:

✔ You may have trouble finding the right word when you are talking.
✔ You may talk on and on without getting to the point.
✔ You may have a hard time understanding and following directions.
✔ You may not understand something if the words do not say it exactly.
✔ You may not know how to use your language skills well when you are with other people. You may have trouble entering or leaving a conversation or participating in a group discussion. You may interrupt other people's conversations because you are not sure when it is your turn to speak.
✔ You may not understand when other kids say something funny or tell a joke.

What can be done?

👍 You may find it helpful to organize some notes in writing before you have to speak in front of a group.
👍 You can ask someone to explain something to you in a different way, if you found it confusing at first.
👍 A speech/language teacher can show you many useful ways to improve your language skills.

5 ☆
WHY DO I HAVE A LEARNING DISABILITY?

The brain is where all learning takes place. It is a part of the nervous system. In the brain there are more than 100,000,000,000 special cells called *neurons*. They connect with each other electrically and chemically. Messages are sent and received by these neurons.

The brain is also responsible for learning problems. When you are learning how to solve a new math problem in school, you need to look at the board, listen to and understand what the teacher is saying, write down the steps the teacher is showing, and remember it all. These steps are done by many different parts of your brain working together.

Because learning is so complicated, something may not go exactly the way it should in the brain. When this happens, the result may be learning problems.

Some learning problems may occur because:

✔ There are not enough neurons to carry some of the messages.

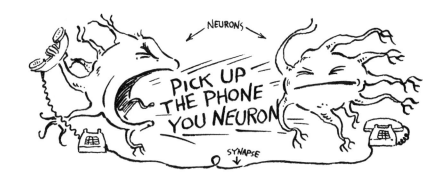

✔ The neurons may carry the messages too slowly.
✔ The neurons may not be connected to each other well enough to send or receive messages.

In most kids with learning problems, many parts of the brain work very well. This explains why you may be very good at learning some subjects, even when you have a hard time learning other subjects.

Many kids with learning disabilities appear to have no problem with the way their brain works. So why do they have difficulty learning subjects such as reading or math? It may be because some brains are better organized to read than to do math. Other brains seem to be organized to do math much better than to read.

To understand this idea, think about the eagle and the mountain lion. Each of them is able to survive in the mountains. The eagle's brain is better organized to understand what it sees from high in the air. The mountain lion's brain is better organized to understand the tiniest sounds it hears from the bushes. Each of these animals has its own abilities and is able to do some things better than the other animal can.

Compensation

Because of the way our brain is set up, if one area does not work well, it is possible to use another area instead. For example, if it is difficult for you to do multiplication in your head, beads or counting blocks can help you get the correct answers. When you use your eyes and hands, different parts of your brain work to solve the multiplication problem. We call this **compensation.** You do what you need to do in a new and better way in order to get the work done. This is why you often need special instruction in the subject affected by your learning disability. The teacher or tutor helps you compensate and find better ways to learn.

Learning Problems

The brain can cause many kinds of problems that make it difficult to learn. You may have some of the following problems, no matter what your learning disability is.

Problems understanding what you hear. These are called *auditory processing problems.* If you have auditory processing problems, you may have difficulty telling similar words apart. You may have problems understanding what you hear. Background noises may bother you, and make it hard for you to listen.

Problems understanding what you see. These are called *visual processing problems.* If you have visual processing problems, you may not recognize differences between shapes, letters, words, or numbers. You may reverse letters, or see the letters in a word in the wrong order. For example, when you see a **b** you may read it as a **d.** You may read the word **was** as **saw.** Some people call these problems *dyslexia.* There are other visual processing problems. You may become confused when you look at a page that has a lot of writing. You may have difficulty seeing all the different letters in a word, especially when the word is long. You may skip words when you read, or you may lose your place when you are reading or copying.

Memory problems. If you have memory problems, you may have difficulties remembering what you learned. You may take a long time learning the correct spelling of words, math facts, or social studies information. You may also lose your train of thought. You may have difficulties remembering directions if they have several parts.

Problems writing or drawing. These are called *visual-motor problems.* You may have visual-motor problems if it is hard for you to copy words, drawings, or designs. You may have trouble staying on the line when you cut with scissors. It may be hard for you to write neatly.

Problems working quickly. You may be able to learn and produce work well, but only if you have extra time. This is called *slow processing speed.*

Difficulties with reasoning. If it is hard for you to solve different kinds of problems, you may have difficulties with reasoning. You may have trouble learning how to solve math problems. You may have difficulty predicting the end of a story. It may be hard for you to

figure out another way to do something when it does not work the first time.

Problems organizing and paying attention. You may have difficulty being organized and paying attention. These problems are called *executive function disorders.*

These may make it hard for you to plan, get started on your work, stay on task, or finish work. You may forget to do your work. You may lose work you have done. The work you do may turn out messy. You may leave your books or assignments at school when you were supposed to bring them home.

If you have trouble paying attention, get easily distracted, and cannot complete classwork or homework, you may have **Attention Deficit Hyperactivity Disorder (ADHD).** Sometimes ADHD causes you to have a hard time sitting still. You may have a hard time learning and getting good grades. People may think that you have a learning disability. Not all kids with ADHD have learning disabilities, but many do. Kids with ADHD often improve when they receive extra home and school help. Medication for ADHD can also help.

Other Problems That Make It Hard to Learn

Anxiety. Anxiety is what you feel when you are very worried or afraid about something much of the time. It is very hard to worry and learn at the same time. For example, if your parents are getting a divorce, you may worry about what will happen. You may think about it and not pay attention to what goes on in the classroom. Therefore, your grades drop. This does not mean that you have a learning disability. When your home situation improves, and when you feel better, you will have less trouble learning.

Physical disabilities or medical illness. If you have trouble learning because you are unable to see or hear well, or because you have an illness that causes you to miss many days of school, you are not considered learning disabled.

PART II

GAINING CONTROL

6 ☆
COPING WITH
LEARNING DISABILITIES

If you have a learning disability, you share many feelings with other learning disabled children.

You feel **frustrated** when you work hard but still do not get the right answers or good grades. You feel **left out** when you do not understand what other kids already know. You feel **angry** when what you know in your head gets all jumbled up when you try to say or write it. You **doubt yourself** when your progress is slow or comes only in small steps. You feel **confused** when you think you know the answers but get a D on the test. You feel **embarrassed** when you give the wrong answer in class.

But, wait a minute,
STOP!!

These are common feelings, but there are things you can do to help yourself. Then you will feel **happy, excited, satisfied, and proud.**

Learn to Like Yourself

If you feel good about yourself, you have good **self-esteem**. When you have a learning disability, it may be hard for you to keep your good self-esteem. You may be teased or picked on. If you have a learning disability you may ask, "Why me? It is not fair." But this is like saying, "Why am I tall?" or "Why am I short?" or "It is unfair that I have straight hair." This is who you are. And this is the person you will grow to like. Think about this:

**Everyone comes to the world
perfect in his or her own way.**

This includes you. To really believe this, you need to realize how important your own strengths are.

Develop Your Strengths

To feel good about yourself, it is important to concentrate on your strengths. These will carry you through. You might say, "I have a language disability in school, but on the track field I am *really* good." Or, "I can't always solve math problems, but I write great stories."

Develop your strengths. If you are good in gymnastics, work hard on the balance beam or the parallel bars. The world can use good gymnasts and talented gym teachers. If you are good at art, work at drawing and painting. The world needs artists and illustrators. Reminding yourself that you are good at some things will improve your self-esteem.

What if you don't know yet what your strengths are? Here are some things you can do:

👍 Your parents know you better than anyone else. Ask them what they think.

👍 Listen to other people when they give you compliments.

👍 Try doing new things and activities you enjoy. This gives you a chance to learn about yourself.

👍 With your parents, look over old report cards to see what your teachers thought you were good at.

👍 Work with a social worker, psychologist, or psychiatrist. These people have been trained to help you find your strengths and feel good about yourself.

Fight Boredom

Some kids who are learning disabled find excuses not to do things that seem hard. They say, "It is not interesting" or "It is boring." Usually when you say, "It is boring," there is a special reason you feel this way. It may feel boring to you because it is difficult.

When something is difficult, you may not want to keep doing it, so it seems boring. Once you begin to understand how to do something, it usually becomes much less boring.

Since it is hard to keep doing difficult work, you might prefer to play or watch television instead. Your parents, teachers, or friends might think that you are lazy. **You are not lazy just because you have learning problems.** If learning were easy, you would just do your homework or classwork quickly and get it out of the way.

Once you get the help you need, you will probably stop feeling bored, and people will stop calling you lazy.

Keep Going

When a mountain climber begins a climb, he looks up and sees a long, difficult trip ahead. If he believes he can do it, keeps going step by step, and does not become discouraged, he will reach the top. Like the mountain climber, if you are determined and willing to **keep trying,** you will reach your goals.

Instead of using your learning disability as an excuse to do less homework, say to your teacher or parent, "I don't understand this. Please explain it again in a different way" or "I need some help to do this." Then keep trying. And continue to ask for help if you need it. You can usually understand even your most difficult subjects, if you give yourself enough time and do not give up.

Learn from Your Mistakes

A sixth grader who studied for a big social studies test by making himself a pile of notecards got a poor grade on the test. Instead of saying, "I'll never study that way again!" he talked it over with his tutor. She pointed out that he tried to study too many cards each day, and often waited until late in the evening to begin his studying. Together they worked out a plan to help him study better next time.

When something works for you, keep doing it. If it does not work, it may not be right for you. But before you throw away an idea, try to figure out why it was not successful. There is a lot you can learn from your mistakes.

Plan Your Goals

A goal is something you hope to accomplish. Setting a goal gives you something to look forward to. Talk with your teacher and with your parents about the goals that are important to you. Get them to help you set up goals you can handle. Keep the goals simple. Remember to look for *your own improvement*, without comparing yourself to your classmates. Your improvement is the best measure of success!

Pat Yourself on the Back

When you feel that you have improved in something, you should learn to give yourself compliments. Tell yourself how you have improved. Then tell someone important in your life about it. For example, you could say, "I did my homework without help" or "I did better on this math test than on my last one." Remember that work does not need to be perfect to show improvement.

Become a cheerleader for yourself.

7 ★

MAKING SCHOOL EASIER

Find a "School Advisor"

So, your day started with your spelling homework going to another school in your older sister's backpack by mistake, but your teacher does not believe it. Then your *little* brother comes to your class to remind you (in his loud voice) to hand in your trip permission slip, because your mother was afraid you would forget to do it.

Instead of punching your backpack, it might be good to talk to someone who can give you some extra TLC (tender loving care). Your school life will be easier if you can find at least one adult who can help you when you need advice on a school problem or help you get through a bad day. You might get the best support from your **classroom teacher,** because this is the person you spend the most time with in school. School **guidance counselors** are trained to help you work out school problems. Sometimes a **specialist teacher,** such as your PE or art teacher, might be the person you find the easiest to talk to.

No one can help every time something goes wrong, but it is good to know who to go to when you need help.

School Accommodations

When you and your teachers have a clear idea about your learning disability, together you can make changes in how you work. A change made in school to help a student learn is called an **accommodation.**

Many students with learning disabilities spend the largest part of the school day in a regular classroom, where most of their classmates do not have learning disabilities. Teachers in regular classes are willing to take into consideration that children have many different ways of learning. They know that small changes can often make a big difference, so they make accommodations to help their students. For example, they may have you use a different spelling book, or do only the even-numbered math examples on a big assignment, or type your social studies essay on the classroom computer.

If you work slowly, you may need more time to finish tests in school. Perhaps you can answer the test questions well, but only if you get extra time. **Extended time testing** is another kind of accommodation the school can offer you.

Find What Works for You

Before anyone can plan good accommodations for you, it helps to understand your learning strengths and weaknesses. When you know your weaknesses, you can work around them. For example, if it is hard for you to memorize, ask your teacher to give you a **test review sheet** early, so you can begin to study as soon as you know a test is coming. If you learn best by listening, you could ask your teacher to let you **tape-record** a test review lesson in class, so that you can use it at night to study. You are then using your strengths to help you learn.

It can be useful to make a **chart of your strengths and weaknesses.** On a large piece of paper, or on the computer, list your learning strengths. Include the school subjects you do well in and the ways you learn best. In the weakness section, list the school subjects you find the hardest, and what makes learning hard for you. Use the chart on the next page as a sample. Some suggestions are given, to get you started.

When you have written up your own ideas, ask your parents, teachers, and other people who have worked with you, such as your tutor, counselor, speech/language therapist, or occupational therapist, if they have more ideas to add.

When you finish, you will have gained a good picture of yourself as a learner. **You are a very interesting person, aren't you?**

My Learning Strengths and Weaknesses

Strengths

My best school subjects:

Ways that I learn best (examples: by listening, by writing, by drawing diagrams):

The best ways for me to show that I have learned something (examples: talking, writing, drawing, tape-recording):

When I have to do assignments on my own, it is better for me to (examples: break big assignments into smaller parts, work at my computer):

Weaknesses

The subject(s) I need the most help in:

The kind of things that are hard for me to do in school:

When I have to (examples: write, read, do math, do social studies)_____, it takes me a long time.

Other things I want my teachers to know about the way I learn:

Speak Up for Yourself!

It is important to let people know what you need. You usually know what works best for you. Now you need to spread this information around. Here are examples of things you could ask for in and out of school:

👍 Tell your teacher if you have been spending too much time on math homework each night. She might be willing to cut down the amount you have to do.

👍 Let your parents know what kind of notebook binder you need in order to keep your school papers better organized.

👍 Tell your soccer coach what will make you feel more in control during the game. You can work out a special signal that you can use to show that you need his attention or help.

👍 Let your friends know what works for you when you get together, like taking turns deciding what the two of you do each time.

Have these conversations when people have time to listen to you. Think ahead about what you want to say. Explain what you *need*, instead of complaining. Ask only for what the person can do. (So forget that idea about asking your teacher to cancel homework for the rest of the year!) Then be sure to listen carefully to the answers and advice you receive.

Special Classes

You may receive extra help for your learning disabilities by working with a **resource teacher,** either in your school's resource room or in your own classroom. Resource teachers usually work with students alone or in small groups, from one-half hour a week to several hours a day. You may spend most of your school day in a **self-contained class** with a special teacher who works only with students who have learning disabilities. Most of your school subjects are studied in this classroom, although you may also be partly **mainstreamed.** This means that you leave your classroom and go into other regular classrooms for some of your subjects, such as math or PE.

Other Helping Teachers

You may work with other teachers, inside or outside of your school, to get extra help. You may meet with a **tutor** after school or during the school day. Since tutors get to know you very well, they can be very helpful. Tutors concentrate on the subjects that give you the most trouble, and teach you how to study and get better organized. A **speech/language pathologist** helps you improve skills in pronouncing words more clearly, organizing ideas into sentences, listening and understanding, and learning how to use your language skills when you are with other people. An **occupational therapist** helps you improve skills that use your fingers, arms, or whole body, so that you feel more comfortable with movement and other physical activities.

8 ☆

MAKING LIFE OUTSIDE OF SCHOOL MORE FUN

Make Home Your Kind of Place

After a long day of carrying around a heavy backpack, writing until your hand hurts, and sitting too long in one place, it feels good to have a friendly, relaxed place to come back to.

It might not be this bad in your home, but here are some ideas to make life run a little more smoothly there.

👍 Work out an agreement with your parents about how much **free time** you may have each day. You deserve to have some free time to "hang out" or play each day. This may mean that you have to prove to your parents that once you do begin your homework, you will finish it.

👍 Try to work out a time each evening when you know your home will be **quiet.** Some families set aside about an hour each day when the television is turned off and everyone does quiet activities. That may make it easier for you to get your homework done.

👍 Set aside a half hour each afternoon or evening when your parent or another person is available to **help** you. This is the perfect time to ask for help with an assignment that is giving you trouble. You can use this time to work on a big project that needs to be done a little at a time. If you are lucky enough to already be done with your homework, you can use this **parent time** for other activities: read a book together, work on a puzzle, start building a tree house.

☝ When your parents give you instructions to do things, have them also **write them down.** You will not have to try to remember everything later, and they will not feel that you are ignoring them.

☝ Talk with your parents about those times when you want them to "fight your battles" for you and those times when you can manage problems **on your own.** If you received a grade that you thought was unfair, do you need a parent to talk to the teacher or can you start the discussion yourself? If someone is bothering you at recess, are there ways that you can work it out without adult help? It is important to ask for help or advice when you need it, but you can also find ways to manage some situations on your own, so that you become a more independent person.

☝ **Do not compare** yourself to a brother or sister. Some things that they can do easily may not be easy for you, but you probably do other things better than they do. No matter what, your skills will get better as you get older. Remember that you are special: strengths, weaknesses, and all.

Make Good Friends

Your learning disability may make it difficult to get along with others. You may be very sensitive to things that people say. You may not know what to do

when a classmate or neighbor teases you. You may have trouble figuring out how other people are feeling when you look at the expressions on their face or listen to the words they use. If you have difficulty listening to and understanding directions, you may find it frustrating to play games with rules. This could make it hard to find and keep friends. **But you can help yourself become a better friend.** Try some of these.

- 👍 Try to find people who have **similar interests** to yours. That makes it easier to find things to do that you both enjoy.

- 👍 Think of someone you would like to **spend time** with. Then plan ahead to do something together for an hour. If that goes well, next time get together for a longer time. Build up the time you spend together slowly.

👍 Learn to **read faces.** Pay attention to how people look when you say or do something, so you can quickly fix mistakes or apologize when necessary.

👍 Listen carefully when someone is talking to you. Try to look people in the eye. If people say something you do not understand, ask politely for another explanation.

👍 **Take turns.** This includes deciding what to do together, who should go first in a game, or who will put the sports equipment away.

👍 **Practice what to say** when someone teases you. For example: "I go to the resource room so that I can do my work in a quiet place with a helpful teacher." It is also a good idea to think up a few sentences that explain your learning disability. For

example: "Kids with learning disabilities are smart. They just need to learn certain school subjects differently. There are actually millions of people with learning disabilities." Get some help from a parent or counselor on this one. Then if someone asks, you will be ready to discuss your learning disability.

☞ Remember that having a learning disability, wearing glasses, being short, or having freckles are all part of being human. Kids tend to pick on children who do not feel **comfortable** with themselves. Learn to understand and feel good about who you are. If you are comfortable with yourself, other people will be comfortable with you.

A Counselor Can Help

Sometimes it helps to see a counselor or therapist outside of school. You can think of counselors as "feelings doctors." They give you a chance to talk over whatever bothers you in your life. Then they try to help you make changes where you need them. You might see a therapist by yourself, together with your family, or in a group along with other kids.

When you see a counselor, you may do more than just talk. For example, you may act out new solutions to problems. You may draw, paint, or play in order to express your feelings. Counseling helps you feel better about who you are, and helps you learn new ways to take care of yourself.

9 ☆
USING COMPUTERS

A computer is a very helpful tool for kids with learning disabilities. It can help you improve your writing, spelling, reading, and math. It can also help you organize your ideas. And, of course, it can be interesting and fun. If you have ever used one, you know that **the computer does not get upset.** It lets you try the same thing again and again. It lets you skip easily to a new part of a game or a program. The computer is patient. You tell it when to start and when to stop. **You are the boss.** Another good thing about the computer is that you are not timed or graded, unless you ask the computer to do that for you.

Keyboarding

A computer is much easier to use if you know where all the letters and numbers on the keyboard are located without looking at them. Learning to use the keyboard properly is useful if you want to do homework on the computer, and it can be a great help if you have poor handwriting. Most kids learn the keyboard quickly and can type twice as fast as they write. You can keyboard at your own pace and your hand does not get tired as quickly as it does when you write by hand.

The look and style of the letters that appear on the screen of the monitor are called **fonts** or **typefaces**. You can change the font on the computer to make it easier for you to read. If you like bigger, bolder type when you read, you can set the computer to that style.

There are many computer programs that teach you how to use the keyboard. But to learn, you will need a practice plan. Try this one: Pick three days each week that you will practice your keyboarding skills for at least 15 minutes each time. Remember: the more you practice, the better and faster your keyboarding will get!

Word Processing

Word processing programs let you correct and change what you write on the computer. With the push of a key, you can correct your mistakes. Your computer can check **spelling** and **grammar.** It can help you create an **outline** to organize your ideas before you begin writing. You will feel good about the work you hand in, because it is neat and easy to read. Your teachers will also be impressed by your work. This makes everyone feel good!

Other Software

Reading and **math** programs can teach you in an entertaining way. You can spend as much time as you need, and then move ahead when you are ready.

Organization programs help you keep track of assignments, due dates, special activities, and reminders. You can use some software programs to make up your own **study guide** when you prepare for a test. Just typing in the information may help you to memorize better. Best of all, when you prepare your own study notes on the computer, you have something clear and easy to read (and you can always go back and print a second copy if the dog eats your first one!)

Some computer programs help you create a **map** or **web** to organize what you want to say. It is then possible to change your information into outline form. You can use these techniques to write an organized paragraph. (See page 63 for an example.)

Think of any math, reading, writing, and organi-

zation software that you already have available at home and school. Don't leave them on the shelf—use them!

With **word prediction** software you type in the first letters of a word, and it predicts, or guesses, words that might fit into your sentence and that start with these letters. For example, if you type in **br,** it might guess the word **brush** if that would fit in your sentence. If the correct word is not shown, you type in the next letter. Usually, no more than three letters need to be typed before the computer shows the word you want, spelled correctly.

Other Technology

Voice recognition technology can be used if you find it hard to write down or type what you want to say. This system recognizes your voice as you are speaking, and correctly types your words for you as you say them. **Word recognition** technology is useful when large amounts of copying and changing are needed. Instead of *you* typing from a printed page into the computer, a *scanner* copies the work for you. Then you can make any changes you want: make the letters bigger, add sentences, cut out parts. **Word recognition reading** technology can scan and *read aloud* printed material. The computer does the reading, and you listen, while you follow the words highlighted on the screen.

Laptops

It is now common to see adults on trains, in airplanes, and in conference rooms, working away on their laptop computers. Laptops are also showing up on the desks of students from elementary school through graduate school. A laptop is a good tool for you, because you can carry it around and use it in many different places. Some teachers will even allow you to type your test answers on your laptop.

10 ☆
SCHOOL STRATEGIES

The good news about having a learning disability is that you are smart and capable, so there are many things you can do to help yourself. Here are ideas to help you do well in school and improve your homework skills. Many of these ideas you can use on your own, but some you might want to try with the help of a parent, teacher, or tutor. Of course, you should try out your own ideas, too, since there are so many ways to learn.

These suggestions are divided into categories. Look at the ones that apply to you, and try out the ideas that you think might help you. Come back to the lists anytime, since your learning needs may change as time passes.

Reading

Figuring out new words. Try some of these ideas when you are reading and come to a word that you do not know:

👍 Look for familiar prefixes (at the beginning of words) and suffixes (at the end of words). Sometimes, just by finding those, you may have already figured out most of the word.

Examples: <u>un</u> **cook** <u>ed</u>   <u>re</u> **work** <u>ing</u>

some common prefixes		some common suffixes	
mis-	dis-	-less	-est
re-	de-	-er	-ful
un-	pre-	-ness	-ing
sub-		-ed	-y
		-ly	

👍 Look for small words that you already know, within a bigger word.

Examples: **test** ify   **start** le

👍 Use "word families" to help you figure out new words.

Once you know the word: **cat**
You can easily learn to read: **fat**
　　　　　　　　　　　　　chat
　　　　　　　　　　　　　splat

And you can then figure out: **splat** ter
　　　　　　　　　　　　　chat ter

👍 Look for compound words. (These are words made up of two small words.) At first, what may look like a big new word may really be made up of two words you already know.

Examples: snow/flake, rain/storm

👍 If you cannot figure out a word, try reading the rest of the paragraph to see if it gives you clues to what the word must be.

Example: The monkey carefully peeled the xmreg and popped it in his mouth.

Without ever having seen the imaginary word **xmreg,** you probably guessed it was a type of fruit, in this sentence.

Understanding what you read

👍 Before you begin a reading assignment, look through the pages to find words you may not yet know. Use a dictionary (or another person) to find out what the words mean. Write down the new words and their meanings, and keep them in front of you, so you can refer to them while you read.

This is easier than using the dictionary in the middle of reading.

👍 Use index cards to write a new word on one side and the meaning on the other side. Keep these cards in a box and review them until they are a part of your vocabulary.

👍 Before you begin reading, know your purpose. If you are reading for enjoyment only, you will read differently than if you are being asked to look for specific information.

👍 When you have comprehension questions to answer, look them over *before* you begin your reading, so you will be prepared when you come to that information. Keep the questions and a pencil next to you as you read, so you can write down the answer or the page on which you found it.

👍 "Talk to yourself." As you read, try to state what the main idea is. Write down the most important idea you find on each page or say it into a tape recorder. This will provide a good summary when you have completed your reading.

👍 If you are allowed to write in the book, highlight sentences that you think are important. Put a special symbol (such as a star or check mark) in front of sentences you do not understand, so you can get an explanation from someone when you finish reading.

👍 As you read, ask yourself if what you are reading is making sense. If not, go back and read the section again. If it is *still* confusing, ask for help.

👍 In subjects that are difficult for you, make it a habit to read chapters more than once. You will find more meaning the second time around.

👍 When reading a novel, use a large index card as your bookmark. Keep notes on it of the things you want to remember, such as names of characters and family connections.

👍 When the book has a long description of something, try drawing it so you can see it better in your mind. For example: the way a character looks, the design of a house, a family tree.

👍 Try using large-print books or tape-recorded books. Listening to a book while you follow along on the page with your eyes may make it much easier for you to understand. Many kids learn better when they use more than one sense (sight, hearing, touch) at a time.

👍 Practice! Practice! The more you read, the more new words you learn, and the easier reading becomes. Start with books you find slightly easy, to build your confidence. Then explore the many other books that are waiting for you.

👍 Read about things that interest you. Sports statistics, beauty tips, and mysteries—any subject you really like will hold your attention as you read, and help you get more reading practice.

Writing

👍 If you have trouble knowing how to begin what you want to say, dictate your ideas first or say them into a tape recorder. Then you can begin organizing them and fixing them up.

👍 "Webbing" or "mapping" before you write your paragraph helps you organize your ideas without having to do too much writing at first.

Here is an example of a web:

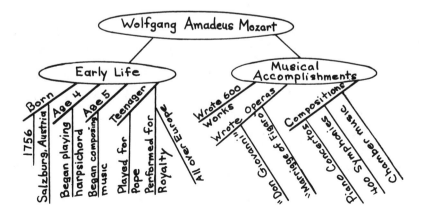

There is no need to write full sentences, since this is just a way to put down your ideas. You can then use this information to form a paragraph.

☞ Remember that every paragraph should contain one main idea, and sentences that give details about your main idea. Here is a paragraph written using part of the web above.

> The musical genius Wolfgang Amadeus Mozart was born in Salzburg, Austria in 1756. At a very young age, Mozart began to show his musical talents. At the age of four, he learned to play the harpsichord. At five, he began composing music. The young Mozart traveled around Europe, where he played music in front of the Pope and members of royalty. His audiences were amazed at the performances of this gifted young musician.

☞ Simple outlines can help you get organized before writing a paragraph or essay.

☞ If you have problems writing down what the teacher says, ask if a classmate can be a note-taker for you. Some teachers will make a copy of another student's notes, so that you can have your own set to take home. Work this out ahead of time with your teacher.

Oral Language

👍 If you have trouble understanding the teacher's directions, you may work out a plan for a classmate to explain them to you a second time before you start your work.

👍 Ask your teacher to give you written directions whenever possible.

👍 If you have something you want to remember to tell your teacher or another person, write it down so you will not "lose your thought." You can write it in your notebook or on a piece of paper with a sticky backing and attach it to your notebook or a page of a book you are using.

👍 When you want to explain something, take time to picture it in your mind. Then try to describe it, using your picture.

👍 Try to start your sentence by saying what your subject is (my baseball game, my friend's broken leg). Your ideas will now follow more easily.

Math

👍 When you write out your math examples, use graph paper to keep your numbers lined up in straight columns. Write one number in each box.

👍 Turn lined notebook paper to the side, so you can line up your numbers in the columns.

👍 If your math paper is too crowded with examples,

rewrite them on a clean sheet of paper, where you can s–p–r–e–a–d out and be accurate.

☝ If you have difficulty memorizing math facts, try learning them set to music. You can sing them to yourself into a tape or you can buy ready-made math-and-music tapes. (See Resources at the end.)

☝ Set aside a whole week to learn one family of math facts. Example:

3	3	3	3	3	3	3	
x 1	x 2	x 3	x 4	x 5	x 6	x 7	…etc.

Concentrate only on these, so you do not overload your brain with the other facts until you are ready.

☝ Use a calculator to check your work once you have completed your math problems.

☝ For math word problems, here are some ideas: Underline or highlight the key words that are being asked (example: Find the sum). Estimate your answer before you work out a problem. Read the problem over several times, or read it aloud, so you understand better what you have to do.

Homework

Yes, there is life after homework, but first you do have to get it done. Try some of these suggestions, so that the "H word," **Homework,** does not have to make you scream.

☝ If you have trouble with homework directions, work with a parent or a classmate (by phone or in person) to make sure you know what to do before you get started.

👍 When you get home from school, make a schedule for that night's work. Write it down—people stick to things better that way. Now you will know how much free time you can plug in for the afternoon and evening.

```
4:00 - SNACK / FREE TIME
4:15 - SPELLING SENTENCES
5:15 - MATH WORKSHEET
5:45 - PRACTICE PIANO
6:00 - DINNER
7:00 - WORK ON BOOK REPORT
8:00 - T.V. SHOW
```

👍 It may help you to come home and get started right away on your homework, to get it out of the way while you are still in a "school mood." Or you may prefer to take a big chunk of free time after a long school day, and then begin homework. Try both ways to see which works best for you.

👍 Always try to get at least part of your homework done before dinner, so you do not end up working late in the evening.

👍 Break a difficult assignment into two or three parts. After you complete each part, take a short break before moving on.

👍 Do homework in the part of your house that is least distracting for you. Get away from the television, the telephone, and your whining baby brother. Some kids like to listen to quiet music, so they are not bothered by other noises.

- If you spend time in a daycare program after school, try to finish a few assignments there. Choose the ones that you find the easiest, especially if it gets noisy there.

- If you work with a tutor, ask for help with homework you find hard. If you are unsure of the directions for an assignment, get help with those, too.

- Promise yourself small rewards for completing each assignment. (When I finish my math, I will get a cold drink.) Plan a bigger reward for completing all your homework by a reasonable deadline each evening.

- If you are spending too many hours on homework each night, arrange a meeting with your teacher. Many teachers are willing to reduce assignments if they know that a student's learning disability makes it harder to do certain assignments.

👍 Don't forget that long-term projects and studying for tests also count as homework. So *think again* when you tell your parents you have no homework tonight!

Tests

Studying for tests

👍 When you take notes in class, write only on the first half of the page. Use the second half of each page to write summary notes to prepare for a test. This way you look at the same page when you go over your notes for class and before a test.

👍 Make study cards for yourself. Put a vocabulary word or math or social studies fact you need to learn on the front. On the back, put the definition or answer, so you can test yourself from either side of the card.

👍 Type or write down what you are trying to memorize. Try saying aloud what you are writing as you do it. Or say the information into a tape recorder and listen to it over and over.

👍 Instead of memorizing entire sentences, select key words that you need to learn.

Example: rice   crop   China

👍 Make a word or words out of the first letters of the items you are trying to memorize. This is called a **mnemonic.** Here is an example: Your teacher asks you to bring your M̲ath, E̲nglish, and S̲ocial S̲tudies books. Remember the word *M E S S.*

👍 When possible, try forming a picture in your mind of what you are studying. Then you will be able to recall the image when you need it.

Example: Pluto is the planet furthest from the Sun.

👍 When you study your spelling words, practice by "writing" them in shaving cream or chocolate pudding. Suddenly, you will find that studying can be fun!

👍 Start studying for a test many days before it will be given, so you will feel confident *and* well prepared the day of the test.

👍 Figure out what conditions work best for you when you need to concentrate. You might do better at a desk or spread out on the floor when you study.

👍 Pay attention to the time of day when you are best able to concentrate. If you do better in the morning, try to do more studying on weekends when the mornings belong to you.

Taking tests

👍 Before you start any section of a test, be sure to read directions twice.

👍 If you have trouble with a test question, make a mark next to it, so you will know to come back to it later. Don't let yourself spend too much time on any one question or section.

👍 Once you know how much time you are allowed for a test, figure out how much time you can spend on each part. Spend the first few minutes doing this kind of planning.

👍 If you feel that you have forgotten something you studied, use a blank piece of paper (with your teacher's permission) to write down everything that comes into your mind about the topic. If you relax, the ideas will come back to you. Now, take whatever you *did* remember and organize it.

👍 If you feel nervous when a long test is given, plan ahead with your teacher to take the test one page at a time, or at different parts of the day, or even on different days.

👍 When you begin a test, take a deep breath and close your eyes for a moment. Tell yourself that you studied and will do your best. (Of course, this only works if you really have studied!!)

👍 Use extra time at the end to check your work.

Essay tests

👍 Make an outline before you begin writing your answers. Plan which information you want to include. Write your outline in pencil, since it is easier to erase and change.

👍 If you have trouble writing by hand, ask for permission to type your essay. You can also ask if you can answer the questions aloud by speaking to the teacher at a different time, or by recording your answers on a cassette recorder in another room.

Getting Organized

If you are one of those students who finds three-week old tuna sandwiches on the bottom of your locker, buried under that other sneaker you have been looking for ever since your gym teacher told you not to come back until you have *two* sneakers, you may want to read these suggestions. Although at first they may seem like just more to do, they will make a difference. You

will also save all that time you usually spend looking for lost items!

👍 Set aside the same day and time each week to clean out your notebooks and backpack. Get rid of all the papers that you do not need. Make sure that all the pages in your notebook are in their correct subject section.

👍 Your desks at school and at home should also be cleared out once a week. At home, use folders and file boxes to keep your desk organized. Make sure you keep the supplies that you need in the same place all the time.

👍 Use a homework assignment book. Before you leave school each day, stop and check that homework is filled in for each subject. If there is no homework in a subject, write "none" or put an X in the space.

- Hang a large calendar in your bedroom. Write down reports, projects, tests, and special activities that are coming up. Each night, after you brush your teeth, look at the next three days on your calendar, so you know what to expect.

- Pack your backpack at night, so you do not need to rush in the morning. Pack your notebook and homework *before* you go to sleep. Then you will not have to start each school day praying that your math homework really is in there somewhere, as your teacher stands next to your desk waiting (with that funny look on his face).

- Don't rely on your memory for important things you must do. Write yourself notes and put them where you will see them.

- Always put important things in the same place (sneakers in the left side of your closet, markers in the outside pocket of your bookbag, lunch money in ... You think of a good spot).

- Learn to plan ahead. You can save yourself a great deal of trouble when you do this. Try to do things in a *logical* order. For example, if you will be cooking something from a recipe, check the ingredients you will need *before* you begin the cooking. If you need special materials for a project, make a list *before* you go to the store.

Big projects

Here is a clever way to remember how to manage your time when you have a big project or a test coming up. Dr. Robert McKenzie, a professor who teaches future teachers, created this mnemonic device. Remember the word **DOOMED** the next time you have a big project. Then remember what the letters of the word stand for:

D eadline. When is it?

O utline what you need to do.

O rder the steps of what you will do

M ake time estimations (How long do you think you will need for each part?)

E nter each step onto a calendar

D ouble-check for conflicts (Don't plan to do a big section of a report on the weekend of your soccer tournament!)

Reprinted with permission from "Fostering Independence in Inclusive Classrooms for Students with Mild Disabilities," a paper presented at the National Conference of Council for Exceptional Children, 1995, by Dr. Robert G. McKenzie, Professor of Exceptional Child Education, Western Kentucky University.

CONCLUSION

We hope that you now have a better understanding of what it means to have a learning disability. As you move from grade to grade, remember what inspires every mountain climber: each step you take brings you closer to your goal. When problems get in your way, you have many tools to help you along. When you feel lost, call upon the people in your life who are there to help.

You live in a time when schools and colleges offer special programs to help learning disabled students. A learning disability need not prevent you from becoming whatever you want to be. You have intelligence, you have strengths, and you have people around you who care.

You have everything you need to reach your mountain top.

RESOURCES

Books

Color Me Successful. Coloring book that tells about 42 people who were awarded The Lab School Outstanding Learning Disabled Achievers Award. The Lab School, 4759 Reservoir Road, Washington, DC 20007

Different Is Not Bad, Different Is the World: A Book about Learning and Physical Disabilities, by Sally Smith. Sopris West, Washington, DC, 1994, 30 pages (for grades 2–6)

The Don't Give–Up Kid, by Jeanne Gehret. Verbal Images Press, 19C Fox Hills Drive, Fairport, NY 14450, 1990, 28 pages (for ages 6–10)

If They Can Do It, We Can Too! by Deephaven School Learning Lab. Deaconess Press, 2450 Riverside Ave. South, Minneapolis, MN 55454, 1992, 87 pages

Josh: A Boy with Dyslexia, by Caroline Janover. Waterfront Books, Burlington, VT, 1988, 100 pages (for ages 10–14)

Keeping A Head in School: A Student's Guide about Learning Abilities and Learning Disorders, by Mel Levine. Educators Publishing Service, Cambridge, MA, 1994, 297 pages

Look Inside Your Brain, by Heather Alexander. Grosset & Dunlap, New York, 1991, 15 pages

Me and Einstein, Breaking Through the Reading Barrier, by Rose Blue. Human Services Press, New York, 1985

My Name Is Brain, Brian, by Jeanne Betancourt. Scholastic, New York, 1993, 128 pages

Putting on the Brakes: Young People's Guide to Understanding Attention Deficit Hyperactivity Disorder, by Patricia Quinn and Judith Stern. Magination Press, New York, 1991, 64 pages (for ages 8–13)

The "Putting on the Brakes" Activity Book, by Patricia Quinn and Judith Stern. Magination Press, New York, 1993, 88 pages (for ages 8–13)

The School Survival Guide for Kids with Learning Differences, by Rhonda Cummings and Gary Fisher. Free Spirit Publishing, Minneapolis, 1991, 164 pages

Secrets Aren't Always for Keeps, by Barbara Aiello. The Kids on the Block Book Series, Twenty-First Century Books, Frederick, MD, 1988, 48 pages

Trouble with School, by Kathryn Boesel Dunn and Allison Boesel Dunn. Woodbine House, Rockville, MD, 1993, 29 pages

What Do You Mean, I Have a Learning Disability? by Kathleen Dwyer. Walker and Company, New York, 1991, 37 pages

When Learning Is Tough: Kids Talk about their Learning Disabilities, by Cynthia Roby. Albert Whitman, Chicago, 1994, 56 pages

Audiotapes

Recordings for the Blind and Dyslexic, 20 Roszel Road, Princeton, NJ 08540 (609–452–0606; 800–221–4792). This national nonprofit organization loans recorded books for up to a year. They have a large audio library and are also able to record additional books that meet their requirements.

Rock 'N Learn, P.O. Box 3595, Conroe, TX 77305–3595 (800–348–8445). Audiotapes that help children learn their math facts (addition, subtraction, multiplication, and division facts set to music such as rap, rock, and country tunes).

"Talking Books" are available through many regional libraries when children have the required documentation for their use. For information and application, contact National Library Service for the Blind and Physically Handicapped, Library of Congress, Washington, DC 20542 or your regional library.

Videotapes

I'm Not Stupid. Learning Disabilities Association of America, 4156 Library Road, Pittsburgh, PA 15234–1349

Picture of Success. Learning Disabilities Association of America, 4156 Library Road, Pittsburgh, PA 15234–1349

Reach for the Stars: An Inspiring Story for People with Learning Disabilities. The Lab School, 4759 Reservoir Road, Washington, DC 20007

Other Materials

Organizational Help

Organizational Tools for Students in Grades 3–12. Success by Design, P.O. Box 957033, Hoffman Estates, IL 60195 (800–327–0057). This catalogue contains materials to help students get better organized, including structured assignment notebooks and student calendars.

Spelling Help

Bad Spellers' Dictionary, Second Edition, by Random House, New York, 1995, 216 pages. This reference tool acknowledges the many spelling irregularities that exist in English. The dictionary presents the correct spelling of words, as well as their most common misspellings, to make it easier for the reader to locate them.

Spellex Word Finder, by George Moore, Richard Talbot, and G. Willard Woodruff. Curriculum Associates, N. Billerica, MA, 1995, 128 pages. This book provides a way to locate common words in order to check on their spelling.

A Spelling Dictionary for Beginning Writers, by Gregory Hurray. Educators Publishing Service, 31 Smith Place, Cambridge, MA 02138 (800–225–5750), 1987, 52 pages. A combination dictionary and thesaurus of the words used most frequently by children in their writing. (grades 2–6)

Word Demons—A Spelling Game, by Caroline Peck. Educators Publishing Service, 31 Smith Place, Cambridge, MA 02138 (800–225–5750). A game that helps children learn 86 nonphonetic spelling "demons." (grades 2–4)

Computer Software

Desktop managers

Kid Desk. Edmark, P.O. Box 3218, Redmond, WA 98073 (800–426–0856)

Launch Pad. Berkeley, 2095 Rose Street, Berkeley, CA 94709 (800–540–5535)

Encyclopedias

Compton's Interactive Encyclopedia. Compton's New Media, 722 Genevieve, Suite M, Solana Beach, CA 92075 (800–338–0700)

Encarta. Microsoft, One Microsoft Way, Redmond, WA 98052 (800–426–9400)

Grolier Multimedia Encyclopedia. Grolier Electronic Publishing, Old Sherman Turnpike, Danbury, CT 06816 (800–356–5590)

Foreign languages

Learn to Speak Spanish/French. The Learning Company, 6493 Kaiser Drive, Fremont, CA 94555 (800–852–2255)

Integrated word processing, database, spreadsheet, drawing, painting

Claris Works. Claris, One Microsoft Way, Redmond, WA 98052 (800–628–2100)

Microsoft Works. Microsoft, One Microsoft Way, Redmond, WA 98052 (800–426–9400)

Write Outloud. Don Johnston, 1000 N. Rand Road, Bldg. 115, P.O. Box 639, Waucona, IL 60084 (800–999–4660). This is a "talking word processor" that also contains a talking spell checker.

Keyboard skills

Kid Keys. Davidson, P.O. Box 2961, Torrance, CA 90509 (800–545–7677)

Mario Teaches Typing. Interplay Productions, 3710 S. Susan, Santa Ana, CA 95173

Mavis Beacon. The Software Toolworks, 60 Leveroni Court, Novato, CA 94949 (800–234–3088)

Math

Blocks in Motion. Don Johnston, 1000 N. Rand Road, Bldg. 115, P.O. Box 639, Wauconda, IL 60084 (800–999–4660). Thinking and problem-solving skills are the focus.

Math Blaster: In Search of Spot. Davidson and Associates, P.O. Box 2961, Torrance, CA 90509 (800–545–7677)

Number Munchers/Fraction Munchers. Minnesota Educational Computing Corporation (MECC), 6160 Summit Drive. North, Minneapolis, MN 55403 (800–685–6322)

Treasure Galaxy. The Learning Company, 6493 Kaiser Drive, Freemont, CA 94555 (800–852– 2255)

Organization

Calendar Creator. Power–Up Software Corp., 2929 Campus Drive, San Mateo, CA 94403 (415–345–5900)

Claris Organizer. Claris, One Microsoft Way, Redmond, WA 98052 (800–628–2100)

Inspiration. Inspiration, 7412 South West Beaverton, Hillsdale Hwy., Suite 102, Portland, OR 97225 (503–297–3004)

Side Kick. Starfish Software, 1700 Green Hills Road, Scotts Valley, CA 95066

Reading/language arts

Interactive Reading Journey. The Learning Company, 6493 Kaiser Drive, Fremont, CA 94555 (800–852–2255)

Reader Rabbit 1,2,3. The Learning Company, 6493 Kaiser Drive, Fremont, CA 94555 (800–852–2255)

Reading machines and software for computers that scan written text

Arkenstone, Inc., 1390 Borregas Avenue, Sunnyvale, CA 94089 (800–444–4443). Students can listen to the text being read aloud by the computer at the same time as each word is highlighted on the computer screen.

Simulations

Oregon Trail and Oregon Trail II. MECC, 6160 Summit Drive North, Minneapolis, MN 55403 (800–685–6322)

Sim City 2000 (and the rest of the line). Maxis, 2 Theatre Square, Suite 230, Orinda, CA 94563 (800–556–2947)

Social Studies

Carmen San Diego Series. Broderbund, 500 Redwood Blvd., P.O. Box 6121, Novato, CA 94948 (800–521–6263)

Super Munchers. MECC, 6160 Summit Drive North, Minneapolis, MN 55403 (800–685–6322)

Voice recognition

Kurzweil Voice Recognition Technology, 411 Waverly Oaks Road, Waltham, MA 02154 (800–380–1234)

Word prediction

Co-Writer. Don Johnston, 1000 N. Rand Road, Bldg. 115, P.O. Box 639, Wauconda, IL 60084 (800–999–4660)

—